An Olive Branch for the Conquered

POEMS BY
CHARLES STEWART ROBERTS

CHESTNUT HILLS PRESS
MCMXC

Certain poems have been previously published in *The Journal of the American Medical Association* ("Modigliani, Italian Painter in France"), *The Quarterly* ("Decatur Cemetery," "Vermeer's Head of a Girl," "Vuillard," "Lincoln," "Leaving Atlanta," "After Edgar Allen Poe," "Cassone"), *Mid-American Review* ("Variations on Gauguin," "Marbot"), *Confrontation* ("The First Night," "Kandinsky's Moscow in the Early Morning"), and *The American Poetry Review* ("Cezanne").

Copyright © 1990 Charles Stewart Roberts
Library of Congress Catalog Card No. 90-62642
ISBN 0932616-31-3

For Carey Roberts

"By a world of marsh that borders a world of sea."

The Marshes of Glynn
Sidney Lanier, 1878

Contents

Vermeer's Head of a Girl	7
Cassone	9
The Young Poet	10
Quincy Square	11
Kandinsky's Moscow in the Early Morning	12
Cezanne	13
Variations on Gauguin	14
Modigliani, Italian Painter in France	16
Vuillard	17
Letter From Arles	18
Marbot	19
The Postcard	20
Days of Anger, Days of Prayer	21
Flaubert	22
Ranier Maria Rilke	23
Pasternak	24
Marina Tsvetayeva	25
After Edgar Allen Poe	26
Hart Crane	27
The Death of Delmore	28
Ezra Pound	29
T. S. Eliot of London	30
James Joyce	31
Bayreuth	32
The Unfinished Tenth Symphony	33

Contents

Disraeli of England	34
The Fatalist	35
Marcus Aurelius	36
The Dusty Chandelier	37
Jefferson at Monticello	38
Andersonville	41
Lincoln	43
Prisoner After War	44
Decatur Cemetery	46
The First Night	47
Studies in Composure	48
Pastel Colors	49
A Morning Letter	50
A Departure	51
Four Rose Themes	52
Waiting Room	54
Vida	55
Alla Prima	55
Postscript	56
The Photographer	56
Four Suicides	57
The Deerskin	58
Hommage to Isabella	59
Leaving Atlanta	61
Six Letters to a Son	62

Vermeer's Head of a Girl

I.

This girl with a gold earring
unravels her blue turban
one century at a time

with pink camels casting
a shadow on pyramids
in a pastel beside her.

She is the silent poetry
of color on white canvas
but I will paint her black

cover all her colors
even the milk in her eyes
that washes down my throat.

II.

Whole nights pass without touching.
I sometimes sleep on the last look
wrapped in blue blankets, thinking too much.

She breathes with Arabian rhythm and stares
with Latin morals, saying nothing at all.
Now she looks at the cat asleep on a stack

of journals, at the wall where a family
portrait hangs, and in the doorway
where another woman stands.

She has been quiet for three centuries.
Breathing, I breathe without life.
I wait endlessly for her to speak.

III.

I will live out this love:
bear no trace of her kiss.

She spent six months in Paris
and knows what is her due.

The cracks are already there
in the white paint of her eyes.

Cassone

Proust would have me wait,
Live out these days alone,
Gathering strange knowledges.

And what things I know! English
Poetry since the Boer War,
How to sew a laceration.

It is true, some nights
Are like those of the gods:
I fall asleep with an audacity

Beyond comprehension,
More solitary, more abandoned.
But other nights it incapacitates

Like a first bereavement. I must
Think it out part of the way
And feel my way the rest,

Seeing everything degraded by
Imperceptible degrees and my own
Dreams I do not recognize.

The Young Poet

This winter's night in Boston
I sit alone in my room.
Before me is a teacher
I mustn't leave too soon.

The snow is falling outside,
All footprints covered up.
The sidewalk is deserted,
No one to interrupt.

Outside I'd smell the air,
So clean and full of frost.
I'd wander through the streets,
Recov'ring what I'd lost.

But I mustn't leave this teacher
Who has so much to tell;
I'll sit alone and read
But glance outside as well.

Quincy Square

You complain that I have
cultivated a certain stature
but I must tell you

This old man on his knees
who pulls weeds each morning
by the walls of the nursing

home in which he lives
grows rows of violets and
never looks up as I pass

and while I write at night
young intellectuals play chess
by candlelight at the Square.

Kandinsky's Moscow in the Early Morning

Just as a painter knows
when his city looks
its loveliest, for him
in the early morning
when its colors melt
in a sun still golden

a poet knows with only
half a look at nature
one at an old poem
and ten at his paper
when the sun has turned
red enough to write.

CEZANNE

Women frightened him, even clothed,
but he leaned on his sister who leaned
on Rome, for he knew that in painting
one may come upon something no one
can deal with. First the confusion,
then insecurity, for a long time nothing,
then suddenly one has the right eyes.
He let no one watch him paint, demanding
absolute silence, treating models like
still-life. His goal was the human face.
He made twenty-six portraits of his wife.
Vollard sat a hundred times for one
painting and hardly spoke, fearing Cezanne
would slash the canvas with a palette knife.
When Zola wrote *L'Oeuvre* about the washed-up
painter everyone knew to be his friend,
Cezanne would say, "The goddamn idiot.
Excuse me. I love Zola so much." Rilke
saw all of Cezanne in a few paintings,
the cooking apples and wine bottles
that belong in pockets of an old coat.
From Cezanne he learned to stop writing,
"I love this here." He knew one must live
in one's art and remain there in order
to say with abandon, "Here it is."

Variations on Gauguin

I.

Think of him and his Indian girl
Who was found wandering in the Gare de Lyon
With a card hanging by a string around her neck
                Enscribed "Anna"

How she was sent to him who sought a model
And she pleased him and he kept her

And how on the streets of Montmartre where he walked
With his height and arrogant bearing and a cloak
Around his shoulders, she followed
In a cotton dress of bright color

And then how in Breton, when peasants in their fear
Derided her and claimed she was a witch
Gauguin defended her with stones.

II.

When he went to the earth's ends to paint
The Academy was unaware of his absence
While the women who drove him off
Powdered their faces with the same ochre
He used to paint the flesh of Tahitians.

III.

He ate breakfast
with no thought
of his landlord
who hung himself

in the kitchen
the same morning
telling his friends
that night how
the wife handed
him a knife
to cut the rope.

IV.

I once hated empty walls.
Whom one hangs on the wall is
                        no light matter.
Gauguin hung naked women
In his rooms and got rid of
                        lots of people.

V.

Men who fear other men:
How soon they're forgotten.

When Gauguin said "Vincent"
His voice was gentle

And Degas telling Gauguin
"Your foot is in the stirrup."

To paint freely:
That is not to lie to oneself.

Modigliani, Italian Painter in France

The French had no Dante.
They would never understand his hell.
He was spitting blood before he met his last love
and she killed herself the day of his funeral.
One might believe his genius came late.
He used a sharp pencil, trading sketches for
hashish or brandy, refusing to sign his work.
He avoided Picasso and walked out on Renoir
but liked Soutine, the neurotic Russian, helping him
carry an ox carcass to his studio. An English
woman, Amedeo's first love, left him this note:
"Paint, my dear boy, paint. You are a painter,
aren't you?" He made love to his models first.
Each woman's face he painted like the last.

Vuillard

Lips brought to a point, a whole Spring
spent with one wife in a French parlor
and a potent theory of color.

She hides among apricots and blues,
raspberry and paper-white stripes of a dress
blending with the books.

And his self-portrait presents him
as it should, his hair leaf-yellow,
his eyes bloodshot, behind him black.

Three centuries earlier in the same country
Montaigne would write, "I play the child.
I cannot endure myself."

Letter From Arles

I stand apart from my own life,
Fresh out of madness. The mistrals
Shake my canvas in the fields.

Arguments with Gauguin are savage.
I am dissatisfied with everything I do.
Friends I make into murderers.

The woman to whom I gave my left ear
Has forgiven me. This morning I made
Another in paper mache.

I am still trying to paint wind:
To bend boughs and turn leaves,
Mingle dust in the troubled air.

Marbot

Marbot was only half in this world.
The affairs with Goethe's daughter-in-law
and Byron's mistress had little effect.

He could do without anyone but Shakespeare
whose Hamlet played on the stage of his soul
and Mother, whose incestuous letters

he never burned. "You have the gift
of being diverted by pictures," she wrote,
"I long for age, when all passions are spent."

He roamed Europe alone, admiring the self-
portraits of Rembrandt and Giorgione.
Delacroix painted him in Paris, leaving out

his gold bracelet. "This artist is suffering
from something," he wrote, "I do not know what
and yet I believe I understand him."

He moved from aesthetics slowly into ethics,
discussing death with Leopardi over dinner,
claiming that Schopenhauer disregards the soul.

When he vanished in Italy at thirty, his mistress
discovered one of two dueling pistols missing.
The last entry in his leather volumes reads:

"I shall go to bed at noon. Admittedly
it is not yet noon. But why wait until the sun
is at its zenith. It is not my sun."

The Postcard

The postcard you sent
I have taped to the wall
Beside Manet's Olympia.

The stare of Baudelaire
Is harsh. He said his book
Was not made for women.

Unlike the book
His face astonishes me.
The bones of his cheeks

Are charcoals under the taut
White skin. His hairline
Has receded; what a great

Colorless brow he has
Without a wrinkle,
And yet he frowns.

I know what woman
Hewed his reticent lips
And found his tongue.

Days of Anger, Days of Prayer

> *...the harlots of Baudelaire.*
> Ezra Pound

In days of anger he wept on the bare
breast of his mulatto mistress
and never emerged from himself.

Comparing each scene to the sensation
of opium, he was executioner in love
living three minutes in one.

When his *Flowers of Evil* were judged
obscene, he claimed they were not written
for women or the bourgeois in his stable.

What conversation can a woman have with God
he asked with a shudder of horror
as George Sand tried to abolish Hell.

In days of prayer he wished his mother
a sufficient span of life to see
a change in him that never occurred.

He finally declared in *My Heart Laid Bare:*
"There are three things worthy of respect:
the priest, the warrior, and the poet

to know, to kill, and to create.
The rest are born for the whip."
He was a great man and a saint

according to his own standards
which were all that ever mattered
before the chancres and madness.

Flaubert

When he lunched at the Exposition
in Paris in 1867
he thought of America
and wanted to speak like a slave.

He lived with each novel
like an oyster stuck to a rock
but after *Sentimental Education*
the fascination was gone.

When he had written a description
of the Forest of Fountainebleau
he wished to hang himself
by one of its trees.

Ranier Maria Rilke

He loved Russia
and the Russians licked his boots.

In a dark Tyrolese cape,
Speaking German as no one else spoke it,

He met their best poet who stayed
twenty years under his influence,

carrying Rilke's only letter to him
in his wallet, too ashamed to reply.

Another Russian poet wrote him
to the point of upsetting his solitude.

Rilke stopped writing her from Switzerland
and withdrew his friendship —

more important than any human
relationship was poetry.

Pasternak

For the Revolution he was ill-prepared.
It took him twenty years to understand
what Zhivago summarized in a single day.

As a child he saw street celebrations
on the coronation of Nicholas the Second,
Mother played Tchaikovsky on the piano,

and Father illustrated books by Tolstoy.
With the Revolutionary poets he had little
in common. Without mental privacy,

life was incomprehensible, while the candor
of Mayakovsky propagated like potatoes
in the reign of Catherine the Great.

He became obsessed with Stalin, believing
"The Tsar was a maniac and a murderer,
now it's a pig and a fool." The seasons

of cruelty drove him south, translating
Shakespeare's Lear as quiet as Romeo.
In the end he rejected his own writing.

Of only *Doctor Zhivago* he was not ashamed
and died lamenting the Russian poets
of his own kind who killed themselves.

Marina Tsvetayeva

Her soul was well-bred.
There was nothing of Eve in her.
She wished to have a son by Pasternak
who refused to leave Russia to rendezvous
in London; but of course there were old men,
the old men with beautiful manners,
in whose memoirs she would still rank
at the top, figuring as their first love.

When she moved her family to Vendee,
it was only because of the name — no one
had forgotten Bonaparte. They called her
Russian. She insisted that she was not Russian,
that she was a poet to avoid being Russian,
in order to be everything.

Exiled to Elabuga in forty-one, friendless
and widowed by the reign of terror,
she would remember the blue lips
of the black girl eating violets
at boarding school in Switzerland,
and the blue of Lake Geneva, cracking
gooseberries the color of her eyes.
She hung herself in this poem of the end.

After Edgar Allen Poe

A Russian poet called it the agony
That does not belong to anyone
In particular, the suffering

In the absence of a sufferer,
An empty suspense, unfilled
By a life that still goes on.

Poetry is a heartless art.
It does not spare its accomplices.
He lived, preached, was crucified.

Poe was an awkward man to handle.
A masculine force, a feminine face,
A hearse and hack came for his body.

An American poet takes this deeply
Into himself. Breathe, breathe, breathe.
He must carry its heaviness.

Hart Crane

That morning he leaped overboard
in the Cuban sea, both eyes black
where crew-cut sailors beat him —
Did he feel it done to him?

He had thick lips but thin skin.
Catallus would take a beautiful slave
and pretend she was Lesbia.
Crane could not ignore the ache.

Where he came was infinitely more
receptive than Lesbia and took
the colors of the Cuban sea —
it was not a gate of wrath.

The Death of Delmore

We ordered morphine for this girl
whose leg we cut off above the knee
where sarcoma stuck like barnacles
to the rudder of some nameless boat.

Today she lay motionless in her fear
and phantom pain at the foot of the bed,
her father leaning over the rail
in his tweed and terror.

Tonight I am reading Delmore Schwartz
who wrote of pleasure in beautiful phrases.
I am also to my own heart merely a serf.
Why did you self-destruct?

Ezra Pound

It is enough to confess
That his songs quicken the blood,
At once direct and disconcerting.

Kept in a cage in forty-five,
He fenced an imaginary opponent,
His eyes green as a blade of grass

His clinched hand, blue with vein
Here, bone white there, believing
Anyone worth a damn is irascible.

T. S. Eliot of London

Friends fed him gin so he would talk,
But even Frost walked away with a bad taste.
While he searched for order in Paris,
Gauguin's "Yellow Christ" hung in his room.
Of no occupation at twenty-six, he married
and went to his doom. He applied green facial
powder to accentuate the despair and studied
the clinic notes on his wife at the sanitariums.
He loved pain but feared humiliation.
At thirty-four, "The Waste Land" appeared
and Eliot became an editor, advising poets
to focus all their gifts on one poem.
He despised democracy and found America
worm-eaten by Roosevelt liberalism.
California he considered the worst.
He detested the telephone and foresaw
the dominance of technology. "We have
so little time," and he quit the *Criterion*
with England on the verge of war.
For post-war fame he was well-prepared.
There were few surprises, minor eccentricities —
the same tailor, the same tobacconist,
the same freeze and thaw of relationships.
He was always recommending caution.
At sixty-eight, he married his secretary
who nursed him through eight years
of emphysema, while he played solitaire.
She took his ashes to East Coker.

JAMES JOYCE

His back turned to the public,
He spoke in archaic Italian
to his son who had beautiful girlfriends
and daughter who went irreversibly mad.

He wrote *Ulysses* with eyes open
though the light hurt. "Work in Progress"
he wrote with his eyes closed. By then
he carried the white cane of the blind.

Finnegans Wake he called "a mountain
I am boring into from all sides without
knowing what I'm going to find." Later
he compared it to "a little Negro dance."

Days when he could scarcely see he judged
people by their voices. When he analyzed
the rise of Hitler without emotion
his wife came at him with a knife.

Catholicism he called "a beautiful lie."
"Wait until Finnegan wakes," he urged his
Jewish friend who stayed in Paris, out-
lived him, and died in the Nazi camps.

BAYREUTH

"I know little of my own age," Wagner told
Nietzsche, "and my music is untimely.
Having gotten myself so cordially hated
The only think to do is make myself feared."

Nietzsche made twenty-three visits to Trisbschen
Yet Wagner still doubted his loyalty. Belladonna
Soothing his eyes, Nietzsche wore smoked glasses
In the Swiss sun, writing to his sister:

"Really, no one shall force me to do anything."
He left Bayreuth before Wagner's festival was over
And reached his verdict in the Bohemian forest:
This composer degrades his muse to a whore.

The Unfinished Tenth Symphony

The humility of men towards men hurt him.
By twenty-eight he heard roaring in both ears,
Confined himself to a room and never gave
A lesson or concert. He composed at his desk
With the piano locked, hearing the full
Orchestra. Eroica was written for Bonaparte,
Not for the Viennese he lived with and
Detested. They cared only for horses and
Ballerinas, and the poets were of little use,
Even Goethe was too fond of court air.
At fifty Beethoven was arrested as a tramp,
His skin jaundiced, his teeth dazzling white.
He had no wife to be in love with him.
A bogus diamond ring sent by the Prussian King
He sold to buy white wine from the Rhineland.
His unfinished tenth symphony was for a people
He admired for their simple manners — the English,
Who sent a hundred sterling to his death bed.

Disraeli of England

Watteau-like women criticized him well.
He learned never to explain or argue,
How to speak with self-possession,
That love endangers marriage.

In Gibraltar he changed canes at noon.
From Venice he took home Byron's
Gondolier, confessing early
"I wish to act what I write."

Years later the jewelry disappeared.
He dressed only in black and married
A widow thirteen years older. Dante's
Inferno remained his consolation.

The Fatalist

> *"Not as that dream Napoleon…"*
> Auden

Turning Catholic, he finished a war in the Vendee.
Turning Muslim, he established himself in Egypt.
Turning Ultramontane, he won the Italian mind.
If his people were Jews, he would have rebuilt
          The Temple of Solomon.

In exile, his pen became a sword.
But he knew enough not to write in a rage,
Except to Josephine, to whom he wrote:
"I arrive at Milan, I rush into your apartment,
I have left everything to see you, to press you
Into my arms… You were not there."

In Moscow the snow ruined him.
From there he returned a fatalist.

Marcus Aurelius

These pages bound in leather
beside Frost and the French yellow sofa
have a life unattached to life, as their
author had in Rome — no one reads them.
He spoke of this fire in which we burn,
pacing the palace floors half-naked,
to himself, "You burn because you bathe
at unreasonable hours, you're too curious
about what you eat, you care too much
for the color and texture of your clothes,
you notice the beauty of your slaves."

The Dusty Chandelier

The blue paint of her husband's suit
Is cracking like the brown leather
Of his Confederate memoirs, shelved
In confusion, the grandfather clock
On the dinner hour for decades.

Edward giving up the British throne
Was the world event of her lifetime.
"War, of course, was different,"
And the unseemly decline of each sister,
"Honey, you learn after so many years

There are things worse than death."
I am reading an author's inscription:
"To Ruby Roberts, who has stood as
A model to me of what the true Southern
Lady should be," my cyclothymic mother

Charming her aging, altogether different
Mother-in-law, who is now setting
The silver for two in the dining room.
I begin this book and await the bell
For dinner under a dusty chandelier.

Jefferson at Monticello

I.

He wrote in private,
Ten books on the floor,
A large Bible on the sofa,
Fruit on a plate.
He avoided the kitchen,
Except to wind the clock,
Drank water and wine,
Sometimes cider from red
Apples cleaned one by one
By the house servants
In two summer weeks,
Ate vegetables, animal
Food only as a condiment,
Dressed plainly and simply,
But perfectly neatly, never
Danced or played cards,
Spoke without profanity,
Bowed to everyone he met,
Fixed his own fire
And covered it carefully
When he left his room.
He lived temperately.

II.

He had six children.
His wife died at thirty-three,
Obtaining his promise not to bring
Home a stepmother to the only two
Surviving children, both girls.
Maria married John W. Eppes,
Had one son survive past

Infancy, then she died.
Jefferson gave him lands
At Poplar Forest in the will.
Martha married a Randolph
And went to Edgehill plantation.
Thomas Jefferson Randolph, their son,
Assumed the affairs of Monticello
In the last decade in the life
Of Jefferson who advised him
To keep account of everything.
Nothing was too small to record.

III.

He did not drink the Antigua rum
Kept for the servants at Monticello.
The father of Betty Hemings, a bright
Mulatto, was an English sea captain,
Her mother an African slave. She bore
Twelve children with four fathers.
The youngest was nearly white.
In his will, Jefferson freed
Joe Fossett, an ironworker,
Burwell, the painter and glazier,
And John Hemings, the carpenter,
Who helped build his University.

IV.

Before he left he knew the names
Of all the trees at Monticello.
After two terms in Washington, he wrote
To Pierre Samuel du Pont de Nemours:

"Within a few days I retire to my family,
My books, and farms... Never did a prisoner
Released from his chains, feel such relief
As I shall on shaking off the shackles
Of Power... I leave everything in the hands
Of men so able to take care of them
That if we are destined to meet misfortunes
It will be because no human wisdom
Could avert them." When Washington was burned
By the British, he sold six thousand books
In pine boxes carried by sixteen wagons
To restart a Library of Congress. Once a year
He went to Montpelier to visit Madison.
Entertaining at Monticello consumed so much
Income he spent summers at Poplar Forest.
He never came out before breakfast. In the cool
Of an evening, he worked in the garden.

Andersonville

> *Cruelties have been committed at Andersonville;*
> *some one has to suffer for it; they have me;*
> *therefore, I am the one, voila tout.*
>   Captain Henry Wirz, C.S.A.
>   Diary, October 6, 1865

Mere thought of the accusations
made him shudder. Under the dome
of the nation's capitol

a military commission sat
"without regard to hours"
and found him guilty.

The terms of surrender
agreed to by Sherman and
Johnston were disregarded.

Witnesses summoned by the defense
were dismissed by the prosecution.
He was doomed before the trial.

Condemned to hang,
he wrote from Old Capitol Prison
to the New York Daily News:

"My conscience is clear.
I have never dealt cruelly
with a prisoner under my charge."

Volumes of invective were published
to vent the Northern spleen.
The Swiss embassy ignored him.

For six months he waited,
appealing to Johnson in the end:
"Pass the sentence...

The pangs of death are short,
and therefore I humbly pray
that you will pass your sentence

without delay. Give me death
or liberty. The one I do not fear;
the other I crave."

He was promised a pardon
if he would implicate Davis,
an offer he rejected with scorn.

Three months earlier in the Daily News,
an officer on Sheridan's staff saw
"an olive branch for the conquered

not a hangman's noose...
let it never be said than an American
soldier, whether Northern or Southern,

could deliberately assassinate
thirteen thousand defenseless men,
trusting to him alone for protection."

Denied a Christian burial,
the body was laid beside conspirators
in the assassination of Lincoln.

LINCOLN

Gunshots at Ford's Theatre
Frenzied the Northern mind.

He was a private man, even
In the disturbance of war,

Writing cursive to the mother
Of five killed soldiers:

"How weak and fruitless
Must be any word of mine

Which should attempt to
Beguile you from the grief

Of a loss so overwhelming."
It is simplicity which saves.

The blue ink of his pen
Separated him from madness.

Prisoner After War

> *"We had only silver on our tongues."*
> Jefferson Davis

Breathing air drawn through iron bars,
His reticent lips quoted Milton,
The tongue red with rust.

He read Macauley's *History of England*,
Marking passages with his fingernail;
His South was Cromwell's Ireland.

Locks of hair he sent to his wife
Waiting under watch in Savannah
With her opiates and children.

Human eyes fixed on every movement,
He compared himself to Lafayette,
And spoke French to his fellow

Confederate Clay, by whom he passed
during daily walks with guards
on the ramparts of the fortress.

Weak brandy and water was served
With his cut-up food and spoon.
No knife and fork were allowed him,

"Lest he should commit suicide."
Insomnia and the Psalms went with him.
A Catholic bishop in Charleston

Turning from the wounded woke him
Every night, "This war, Mr. Davis,
This war. I am heart-sick, heart-

Sick, heart-sick," while the foot-falls
Of a Pennsylvania officer echoed,
Rendering the revenge of a nation.

Decatur Cemetery

I was struck less by the gravestones
In the field through which I passed
Than by the manner of three squirrels

Who had toppled over a clay pot
Of yellow roses, crushed the blossoms,
Begun to nibble on their petals

And who, as I passed by, dashed behind
The gravestone of a colonel who served
Georgia and died in one of the wars.

The First Night

The first night she read Sylvia Plath,
"You do not do, you do not do any more,"
as if she knew her father long enough
to finish him. We smoke cigarettes
and wore sweaters all shades of brown.
I lay beside her when her friend called
from England, leaving when I heard her
laugh. Two years later she still speaks
to me as if to herself, "There are these
red stopsigns in my head. You and I
understand each other, don't we?"
There are these yellow fields of paper.
Nothing else occurs to me. I do not wish
to understand. She exhausts me.

Studies in Composure

I.

When Roethke was weary of women,
He drank whiskey and desired God.

Now at breakfast I eat my melon
With no thought of her desires.

They say I am happier than ever,
With no designs on her quiet.

II.

Beyond fire and the poets
   With savoirfaire
And women who want romance

There is my winter:
   I drink iced bourbon
From a Jefferson cup

To celebrate the cool
   Wood-ash in my hearth
And burn like these lines.

Pastel Colors

Where I must walk
The pastel colors are fading.
You come in from outside and rub

Soil into the blues and apricots
With James Joyce staring at you.
I framed him for this reason.

And Napoleon with a sabre
Who sees the great fall
Of ashes near the fireplace.

We have many fires. The creams
Have already gone cloudy.
The beige is grey with smoke.

I must turn the rug over soon.
The cat has begun to claw
The apple green design.

A Morning Letter

There was the tedious and the charming
In the Orient, centuries before Christ.
Less was spoken, more was written.

The gentleman would decorate his carriage.
He would send cakes to the lady-in-waiting,
A red plum blossom attached.

She would reply in poetry,
Spreading her verses in all directions!
The gentleman would take note of her hand.

And if his flute was left by her pillow?
He would send a messenger for it.
She would wrap it like a morning letter.

A Departure

I looked the heart in the eye
this alone was not enough

closed my eyes on day itself
but night was not enough

became a poet all over again
self-possessed but not enough

letting the love live on words
knowing lips are not enough

letting the words speak simply
and die if not enough.

Suddenly I shall leave.
Bearing this will be enough.

Four Rose Themes

I.

She keeps this secret from others:
When she takes to her eyes a rose
It whispers things a lover would.

I have told her my secrets, save one
Which I keep from the highest gods:
If she is alive when clay covers

The closed lids of my brown eyes
I will break the ground again
To look on her with red petals.

II.

"We are opposite in our ways.
Your ideas are of a different century,
Full of certain, almost haughty.

Your actions seem without bounds.
My ideas are easy, open, and tolerant,
And discriminate less than yours."

And all the while his eyes
Explored the details of this rose
Which, when she finished speaking,

He took from the water
In the slender glass vase
And ate, to her abashment.

III.

She walks down the white line
Between the cars, offering roses
Wrapped in green paper. Most of the men

Look away from her, but sometimes
One calls here and she still
Delights in the brief exchange.

On hot days when exhaust burns
The white of her eyes red, she splashes
Upon her eyelids the cool rose-water.

She complains never of this, only once
To her God that none of the ancient
Odes of Cathay were ever sung to her.

IV.

When, in the final analysis,
He realizes that he is not
Nor ever was realistic

To presume that once, just once,
Destiny would yield to will,
Poetry presents itself

And the moon becomes a seed,
Flesh becomes the soil,
And blood becomes a rose.

Waiting Room

She had nothing else to recommend her,
Save the indifferent silence she kept,

But I questioned and she answered
And we became unseemly intimate.

I should have merely nodded when she
Came and left. I would have got me

A pen with just the right point
Some blue Indian ink and maple paper

And written three sonnets before the air
Gave up the fresh scent of her clothes.

VIDA

The Persian girl in blue earrings
The color of her Laura Ashley dress
Speaks with her hands and breasts
Of Milton, mirth, and melancholy.

I follow her movements in the dim
Light of my living room and imagine
A black silk veil across her face.
How her dark eyes follow my stillness!

ALLA PRIMA

Lobster shells crack between cold steel tongs
As the cream-white breasts of this woman
In a low-cut black evening gown
Swell, ever so slightly, with each breath.

Postscript

But then if I sit at a desk
In the far corner of a library
At dusk while people are rushing home

And read poems by Michelangelo
I can be overwhelmed by a loneliness
That quells even the pulse of my blood.

The Photographer

For five minutes this old man
curled up asleep on the concrete
became an object of the enthusiasm
of a young man with a camera.

What is worse: the photographs
will sell in Cambridge as art.

Four Suicides

> *"...and what is mine end, that I should prolong my life?"*
> Book of Job, 6:11

One condemned something in herself.
Another was hiding from chaos around her.
One could not look on his sleeping child.
One did not think it was the end.

The Deerskin

I have held a pen poised
An inch above paper
Well into the morning

Having forgotten the name
Of this Mexican who gave me
The deerskin that covers

The bedside table.
He was the Catholic bishop's
Butler, unmarried, quiet.

The night we arrived in Tepic
He served us rice pudding
In the bishop's dining room.

The next day he led us
Up this black mountain of molten
Lava, cooled by a century of rain.

I fear bad dreams. The bedside
Lamp illuminates the least
Troubling thing

My eyes have set upon tonight:
A bullet hole in the brown
Skin of the deer's neck.

Hommage to Isabella

It deserves a rather long look,
Your painting of Isabella of Portugal
In the spring of her solitude.

My own generation is vulgar.
Yours went quietly and quickly
Like your Nazi lover to Russia

Leaving you and all the music
In Munich. "You may stay here
One more week," the consul said

And back to St. Louis you came,
Broken like the chains of Versailles.
Your old friends? Very knowledgable

About ugly things you thought,
And married a man from Grosse Point
Who compares Germans to lice.

In your hand you collected
Fallen leaves in the garden pool
And described your brother's death:

The urgent flight to England
Driving to the London hospital
With Graham Greene's brother,

The consultation with DeBakey
By telephone, the arrival of a son
Minutes before your brother's death.

All the Loves die quietly
And quickly you said proudly,
Planning your own. And yet at night

I know you read Beaudelaire,
The slow course of whose death
Is a study in misery.

Leaving Atlanta

for W. Clifford Roberts, Jr.

What the teamsters must think
Staring at you when you open
Your Italian leather coin purse.

I will not forget your discomforts:
The Aunts in Grandmother's kitchen,
Janie's manner on the phone,

The Confederate graves at Oxford,
The woman in Cabbage Town
who rolled her tongue at us.

I will remember the Dutch ships
On your wall and the portrait of Booker,
My poems at your bedside.

I will use the sterling knife
You gave me to open letters,
Even if you never write.

You knew my weaknesses.
You never cursed in my presence,
Leaving me to curse myself.

Six Letters to a Son

I.

Your winter of eighty-two in Boston:
The Darsee affair, your first poems,
The girl in Memphis no longer available.

I am thinking of that poem,
"And You, Andrew Marvell..."
I am sure the pain will soon pass.

You will no doubt love many times.
As George Sand wrote to Flaubert,
"I kiss the diamonds on your face."

II.

Beautiful days here!
Lots of trick or treaters.
I remember the lion mask when you were four,
      A lion with a yellow mane.

Warren took down his fort
and the tent he's been sleeping in...
I enjoyed your paper on Dryden so very much.

III.

This has been a strange and exhausting winter,
Warren calling with his whispered words
of anger and despair

Lots of fires in the fireplace.
I need to get back to the book.
So hard — I wake up full energy,
fade out by evening. No one
to talk poetry with.

Am reading *The White Hotel,*
fascinating and erotic.
Will send it to you —
I think!

At my desk in the rose study,
Cool breezes outside...
Where is spring?

IV.

Sometimes things stood out so clearly:
boring dialog, cutesy writing, ponderous prose.
Amazing how one can edit so easily and miss
the same mistakes in one's own work...

I also read Keats, Byron, and Shelley
in my twenties, and many biographies.
I used to be terribly idealistic.

Am less so now. I live so much
in my own inner world that I miss
some of the subtleties. Conrad Aiken,

there was a tragedy. His father shot
his mother and then himself and the boy
was taken north to live with relatives.

V.

A quarter of a century birthday!
How shall we celebrate?

Spain was languid, white, and beautiful.
Mountains of Africa across Gibraltar Straits.
Wondering if you have heard from Melanie...

I keep thinking of you as a young Confederate
at Wilderness or at Gettysburg—maybe
a cavalry officer with high dusty boots,
a dashing but travelworn steed,
an old darkey valet who follows
behind you from camp to camp.

VI.

Butterflies on the beach
and pelicans in the dunes.
Woke to a thunderstorm
      with lightning in the marsh.

I am writing down my dreams.
The book is coming. Am undecided
      how it will end.